Animal  Lives

WHALES

Sally Morgan

QEB Publishing, Inc.

QEB

Copyright © QEB Publishing, Inc. 2005

Published in the United States by
QEB Publishing, Inc.
23062 La Cadena Drive
Laguna Hills, CA 92653

This edition specially created for
Books Are Fun 2006

Library of Congress Control Number:
2005921286

ISBN 978-1-59566-308-5

Written by Sally Morgan
Designed by Q2A Solutions
Editor Tom Jackson
Map by PCGraphics (UK) Ltd

Publisher Steve Evans
Creative Director Louise Morley
Editorial Manager Jean Coppendale

Printed and bound in China

Picture Credits

ardea.com: Francois Gohier 6, D Parer & E
Parer-Cook/Auscape International 23,
Corbis: Paul A Souders 1, 30, Sanford/Agliolo
4, Brandon D Cole 17
Ecoscene: Phillip Colla 10, 24, 27
FLPA: Frank W Lane 7, NORBERT WU/Minden
Pictures 8–9, Gerard Lacz 11, Sunset 15, Flip
Nicklin/Minden Pictures 20, 21, 22, 25
Getty Images: Front Cover Stone, Thomas
Schmitt/Photographer's Choice 13, Darryl
Torckler/Stone 16, Docwhite/Taxi 18–19
RSPCA Photo Library: Mark Votier 29
Still Pictures: Kelvin Aitken 5, 30, Gerard Lacz
12, F Gohier 14, MARILYN KAZMERS 26, Ron
Giling 28–29, BIOS 30

Title page: Humpback whale

The words in **bold** are
explained in the Glossary
on page 31.

Contents

Whales

The largest animal in the world is the blue whale. The blue whale is just one of many types of whales that swim in the world's oceans. Whales are close relatives of dolphins and porpoises.

Whales often leap out of the water. This is called **breaching**.

Whales have flippers, a long body, and no back limbs.

Vital Statistics

The blue whale is the largest animal that has ever lived on Earth. It grows up to 100 feet (30 m) long and weighs as much as 150 tons—that's the same as 20 African elephants.

Whales are not fish

Whales are **mammals**. Mammal is the name given to any animal that produces milk for its young. Whales are unusual mammals, because they live in the water but still breathe air. All mammals have at least some hairs on their bodies. Whales are almost hairless, with just a few bristles in their nostrils.

5

Whale types

There are about 50 different **species**, or kinds, of whales, which are divided into two groups. One group is the baleen whales. This group includes humpback whales, gray whales, and fin whales. Baleen whales have huge plates hanging from their jaws instead of teeth. The plates strain food from the water.

The humpback whale swallows a huge mouthful of water and fish as it comes to the surface.

Toothed whales, such as this beluga, have small teeth that they use to grip fish and other prey.

Toothed whales

The other group is called the toothed whales. This group includes sperm whales, pilot whales, narwhals, and orcas (killer whales). They are smaller than the baleen whales and do not have plates in their mouths. Toothed whales are **predators** and hunt fish, squid, and seals.

Whale

The adult beluga is a white whale, but its young are born dark gray. The young, called calves, turn white by the time they are five years old.

fact

Where can you find whales?

Whales are found in all the oceans of the world, including the coldest oceans such as the Southern and Arctic Oceans. Some whales live in very deep water, where it is pitch black. Many whales swim long distances each year, from cold waters to warmer places and back again (see page 26).

Orcas are found in all the oceans of the world, although they prefer the colder water.

Whale

Narwhals are found farther north than any other whale in the Arctic. They come together to form huge groups of several thousand.

fact

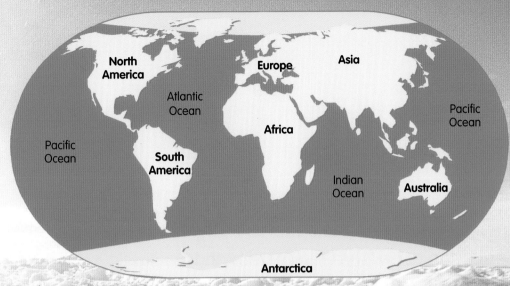

■ Areas where whales are found all year.
☐ Areas where whales are found at certain times of the year.

Cold-water food

Many whales live in **habitats** with cold water. This is because cold water is rich in food for whales, especially krill and plankton. Krill are shrimp-like creatures that grow to about 2 in. (5 cm) long. They are eaten by the baleen whales. Plankton are tiny animals and plants that float in the water. Some whales eat plankton, but plankton is also food for the fish that are eaten by toothed whales.

9

Giving birth

Female whales may be **pregnant** for between nine and seventeen months, depending on the species. Many female whales swim to a special place where they give birth to a single **calf**. As soon as her calf is born, the mother pushes it to the surface for its first breath of air.

Calves of the larger whales, like this humpback, are about 13 ft (4 m) long at birth.

The calf stays close to its mother's side for the first month or so.

Whale calves

The female whale feeds her calf on milk that is rich in fat, so it grows quickly. The calf has to learn how to breathe without swallowing water and also how to stay upright in the water. The calf practices swimming and, after six weeks, it can do a complete roll underwater.

Whale

Female California gray whales give birth in the shallow waters off the coast of Mexico. The shallow water is thought to protect the calves from sharks.

fact

Growing up

Whale calves drink their mother's milk for up to a year. Then they start to eat adult food. This is called **weaning**. Calves are very playful and love to jump out of the water and smash down with a loud splash. They roll in the water and slap the surface with their fins.

Young orca whales are very playful. They jump out of the water and twist in mid-air.

A short-fin pilot whale and calf travel close together through the ocean.

Staying close

The calves follow their mother. By staying close, they learn where to find food and which routes to take on long journeys. Some young whales leave their mother when they are weaned, but others stay close by for a long time. Young sperm whales stay with their mother for ten years, while orcas live with their mother as part of a family group, or **pod**.

Whale fact

Young right whales have been seen to breach (jump out of the water) more than 80 times an hour while playing.

Underwater living

Unlike fish and other underwater animals, whales cannot breathe in water. They must swim to the surface to breathe air. Whales do not breathe through their mouth, but through a large nostril called a **blowhole**. The blowhole is on the top of the whale's head. Just before a whale dives under the water, a flap covers the blowhole. Whales can stay underwater for a long time before they have to surface again.

Sperm whales have a huge, square head, which is filled with a waxy substance called spermaceti. This may help them to dive.

When whales come to the surface, they breathe out so hard that a jet of air and water bursts out of their blowhole.

Keeping warm

Whales have to keep warm in cold water. They have a thick layer of fat, called **blubber**, under their skin. The fat traps heat in the whale's body so it stays warm.

Whale

Sperm whales can dive deeper than any other mammal in the world. Most dives are between 1,000 and 2,000 feet (300–600 m), but they can reach at least 6,500 feet (2,000 m). Sperm whales can swim underwater for two hours without taking a breath.

fact

Swimming

Whales have a body shape that is **adapted** for swimming. They have a large head and long body with no back legs. This gives them a smooth, **streamlined** body that slips easily through the water. They have flippers rather than front legs, which they use to steer as they swim.

Whales are pushed through the water by their powerful tails which move up and down when they swim.

A whale's tail has a notch where the two flukes come together.

Pushing through the water

A whale's tail is made up of two flat fins, called flukes. The flukes move up and down, pushing the whale through the water. The tail is moved by powerful muscles in the whale's back. The largest flukes are those of the blue whale. They are just under 25 feet (8 m) wide.

Whale

The fastest swimmer of the large whales is the fin whale (the second-largest whale), which can swim at 30 miles (48 km) per hour in short bursts. Normally it swims at about 20 miles (30 km) per hour—as fast as a car drives through a town.

fact

Senses

Whales have well-developed senses that help them to find out about their surroundings. Their hearing is incredibly sensitive. Whales do not have ears on the outside of their heads. Instead there are two tiny openings on the side of a whale's head, which lead to internal ears.

Whales have small eyes and cannot see very well. However, this is not a problem for whales because they often swim in dark water.

The tiny eyes of this blue whale are behind its mouth. Whales are used to living in murky water, where they can see objects only up to about 3 ft (1 m) away.

Echolocation

Toothed whales use a method called **echolocation** to detect objects. The whale sends out high-pitched clicks. These clicks bounce off objects and return to the whale as an echo. By listening to the echoes, the whale can figure out the shape and position of objects, including its prey.

Plankton feeders

The baleen whales eat plankton, krill, and small fish. Hundreds of baleen plates form a curtain hanging from the whale's upper jaw. The whale swallows a huge mouthful of water and forces it through the plates, trapping the food contained in the water. Baleen whales eat a lot of food every day—a blue whale eats up to six tons of food a day.

The gray whale is the only bottom-feeding whale. It scoops up huge mouthfuls of mud from the sea bed which it sieves to find food.

This group of humpback whales has found a shoal of fish and is busy feeding.

Working together

Humpback whales often work together to catch krill and fish. They blow bubbles to form a "net" around a group of their prey. Then the whales swim up through the middle of the bubble net and swallow the food in huge gulps.

whale

The bowhead whale has the largest mouth of any animal in the world—a minivan could drive into it! This giant whale's baleen plates are 15 feet (4.6 m) long.

fact

Giant predators

The toothed whales are all predators. They hunt mainly for fish and squid. Their teeth are small and pointed—ideal for gripping slippery prey. They swallow their food whole or in large chunks.

Whale
Sperm whales often have scars on their sides caused by the suckers and beaks of giant squid, one of their favorite foods.
fact

Pilot whales have sharp, hooked teeth. The hook shape helps to stop struggling fish from escaping.

These orca whales have learnt to swim up to the beach to catch seals. They have to be careful that they don't get stuck in shallow water.

Hunting together

Orcas hunt together in a pack. They are intelligent animals and are some of the fiercest predators of the oceans. They prey on fish and seals, and sometimes the calves of other whales. Many orcas gather off the coast of Argentina from October to April, when the seal pups are born. Orcas hunt in shallow water and catch the pups as they take their first swim. An orca can eat as many as eight seal pups a day.

Communication

Whales communicate in many ways. They make different sounds, such as whistles, trills, moans, and squeals. These sounds travel great distances through the water. Breaching and lobtailing (slapping their tails on the surface) are other ways whales communicate with one another.

This whale is lobtailing. It is sticking its tail out of the water and will slap it on the water's surface to make a loud sound.

24

No one is sure why male humpback whales sing. It might be to attract a female, or to tell other males that they are in the area.

Humpback songs

Male humpback whales can sing! Their song contains up to 30 different sounds and it can last for 30 minutes. When the whale gets to the end of his song, he starts from the beginning again. This can go on for hours. At certain depths, the whales' songs travel for thousands of miles through the water.

Whale travels

Many whales make long journeys each year. They spend part of the year eating in cold water and then swim to warmer waters where the female whales give birth to their calves. This annual trip is called **migration**.

Whales stick their heads out of the water to check for landmarks and to see if there are any other whales around—this is called spyhopping.

Why do they migrate?

Often whales swim to warmer waters because their cold-water feeding areas freeze over. Others prefer to give birth to their calves in warm water. Calves do not have a thick layer of blubber, so they could not survive in cold water.

Whales spend several months in warm water and then they swim back to their feeding areas. The whales swim together in groups and follow the same routes each year. Calves swim with their mother to learn the route.

This blue whale and her calf are migrating along the coast of California to their feeding grounds in the Arctic. By the time they arrive in the cold waters, the calf will have grown blubber.

Whale fact

Gray whales migrate the farthest, as much as 12,700 miles (20,400 km) each year, from the Arctic to Mexico and back again.

27

Whales under threat

Whales around the world are under threat. For a long time, whales were hunted for their oil and meat. So many whales were killed that many species almost became **extinct**. In 1986, whaling was completely banned and the whale population started to increase again. But now some countries want to start whaling again.

Whales sometimes get caught in fishing nets or hurt by the propellers of ships. They need plenty of food, and sometimes people take too much fish and krill from the oceans and do not leave enough for whales and other sea animals.

These people are watching gray whales off the coast of California.

In the past, huge numbers of sperm whales were killed for their oil.

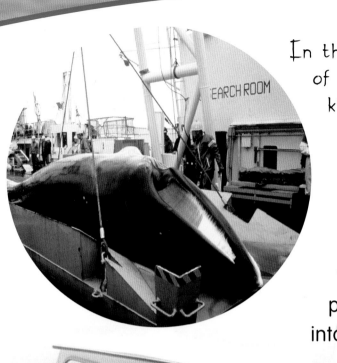

Whale conservation

It is important that whales are protected so that they do not die out completely. Whale watching is enjoyed by many people and brings money into coastal towns, so local people have a good reason to save the whales.

JORGE SCHMID

LW 2568

JORGE SCHMID

Whale

The California gray whale is one of the few animals that has been taken off the list of endangered animals because its numbers have increased enough.

fact

Life cycle

Whales have a long pregnancy, so they only give birth to a calf every two or three years. The calves stay with their mother for up to 10 years. They grow slowly and many are not ready to breed until they are 20 years old. Smaller whales live for about 30 years but the large whales can live for 70 years. Some whales have been known to reach 100 years old.

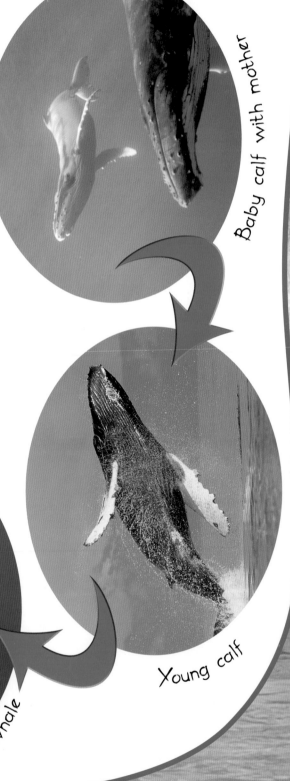

Baby calf with mother

Young calf

Adult whale

Glossary

adapted good for a particular purpose

blowhole the nostril of a whale on the top of its head

blubber a thick layer of fat under the skin

breaching when a whale jumps above the surface of the water

calf a baby or young whale

echolocation a way of finding where things are by sending out sounds and listening for echoes that come back

endangered in danger of dying out

extinct no longer any left alive

habitat the place in which an animal or plant lives

mammal an animal that gives birth to live young, rather than laying eggs; female mammals produce milk to feed their young

migration a journey made each year to find food or to breed

pod a family group of whales

predator an animal that hunts other animals for food

pregnant having a baby or babies developing inside

species one particular type of animal

streamlined having a long, narrow, and smooth shape that slips through water easily

weaning changing from milk to an adult diet

Index